The Acts of Wealth Creation

By

M.P. Mapida

The Acts of Wealth Creation

The Acts of Wealth Creation

CONTENT

INTRODUCTION

As a Business Consultant I have heard a lot of questions like Mr. Sir, How can I be financially free? I want to become a millionaire like you, where do I start from? My job doesn't pay well, I am tired of working for people how can I start my own business?

The fact of the matter is that most people struggle with financial issues and they really want their situation to change but I discovered they are not ready and willing to change their self's. News flash! You are the reflection of your situation, to change it you must start by changing yourself. You have to know what you want and make up your mind to go for it come hell or high water you will pursue until you reach your goal. That determination is very important in beginning the pursuit for success; it will keep you going and help you stand in the face of challenges.

My arm is to open your eyes to the acts and principles of wealth creation, and lead you to the path of successful people.

- How they do their things
- How they react to situations and challenges
- How they invest money and time
- How you too can Become Wealthy

We will be treating all of this in three chapters. So sit tight and read carefully. Follow me closely and I guarantee you will be on the flight to Becoming Wealthy by the end of this book.

In 1917, a 23 year old apprentice at Osaka Electric Company with no formal education came up with an improved socket. But his boss was not interested so young Konosuke Matsushita started making samples in his basement. He later started his own company and expanded with battery-powered bicycle lamps and other electronic products. Matsushita Electric, as it was known until when the company officially changed its name to Panasonic in 2008, is now worth over $70 Billion.

I need you to put it in your head that "age is just a number" and no matter what people may say or how many times you have fail should not deter you from your pursue to succeed in life. It might come as a shock to you, but the man who became what many would call the best basketball player of all time didn't make his high school basketball team. Yeah! *"I have missed more than 9,000 shots in my career. I have lost almost 300 games. On 26 occasions I have been entrusted to take the game winning shot, and I missed. I have failed over and over and over again in my life. And that is why I succeed."* – Michael Jordan.

Whether you are 16 or 60, it is never too late to make your life better. The world is full of infinite possibilities and countless opportunities, but your life and career are finite, meaning you have limited time to find your passion and make your mark in the world.

In the First Chapter we will be treating the 10 Signs of People Who Become Wealthy. So you can re-position yourself if you find out that you are not on track, because what you are trying to achieve has been done by someone in one way or another. The acts of wealth creation are not different, they are one. Our Second Chapter will be to re-tune your mind to the right thinking about money. So you would unlearn the wrong concepts you have about money that has cost you dearly, and learn the right mindset you need to become a success. I call it the 10 Money Ideologies You Must Change. Finally, Chapter Three will seal the deal. It will teach you what to do as a potential multimillionaire. The kind of attitude you should have, the schedule you run and your modus of operandi. I call it the 10 Habits you must cultivate as a Potential Multimillionaire.

Get ready to learn because some of you will eventually run into billions, don't forget to say thank you.

Congratulations in Advance!

CHAPTER 1

10 SIGNS OF PEOPLE WHO BECOME WEALTHY

1) **They choose a career in the area of their passion and gift.**

What motivates people to give a 101% isn't money but passion, and what makes you standout is commitment. So, the question is how much commitment can you give to something you don't love? It is but a little and that is why the people who don't work in the area of their passion and gifts don't standout. They are the ordinary people with extraordinary gifts you see around. Just because of money they have buried their gifts and do not live life to the fullest. Not realising that their gifts and passion are gold mines waiting to be exploited.

Don't put the money first, do what you love and the money will follow. It is a great feeling to get paid to do something you love. Your passion is the strong feeling of excitement you have for something. You can spend the whole day doing that thing without getting bored of it. Something you will do with joy and the whole of your heart even if you aren't being paid to do it. For some people, that thing could be Singing, Painting, Drawing, Fashion designing, Football or probably a Gadgets freak. That activity you drive some much pleasure in doing is your passion.

Mr. Passion is a very close relative of Mr. Gift and most of the time you figure out your passion you will discover that you seem to have special endowment in doing it. Wealthy people leverage on their gifts and passion a lot. In other words they take advantage of it. They don't go to Medical School when they have passion for Music. They don't work in a Bank just because they are in dear need of a job when they have passion for fashion designing. Imagine if Cristiano Ronaldo decided to be a Geographer because Geographers made a lot of money while he was growing up or if Dr. Ben Carson insisted he wants to be an actor if he would have made such remarkable medical history of performing the first completely successful separation of Siamese twins joined at the back of the head.

The first sign of the people who become wealthy is that they choose a career in the area of their passion and gifts. It might be difficult at the beginning but at the long run you will be happy and more successful. Don't put the money first, do what you love and the money will follow.

2) They have a plan.

It isn't just enough to set goals, a goal without a plan is just a dream. I'm one of the people that encourage people to dream really big and set goals that scare them because I know how helpful it can be to your mind. But what is the use of a car without wheels? Of course it is definitely not going to travel even the shortest distance no matter how beautiful or expensive it looks because it lacks the vital part it which it will use to move it beautiful self around. Know it as from today that the wheel that moves your goals is a plan. This reminds me of a popular quote that says, "He who does not plan, plan to fail". Planning involves the use of ideas, inspiration and experiences to provide a work guide for making decisions, aligning priorities and the allocation of resources. Your plan will lead the way and guide the process. It is the road map of your vision. It will help you manage risk and uncertainties, because business has lots of them.

Successful people don't just stop at having a strategic plan for their business or career; they have a plan for their lives. They have clarity of purpose and realistic goals. They don't wake up in the morning and begin to ponder on what to do that day, No, ordinary people do that. They have daily plans, weekly plans, monthly plans, yearly plans and even a life plan. If you want to be successful you must begin to plan.

Have you noticed who all successful people claim busy? You will have to book an appointment and sometimes wait for weeks to see them. People take it for arrogance and pride but in real sense it is a value for time all successful people have. A research was conducted of a recent and you won't believe it, only 6% of wealthy people watch reality shows, compared to 78% of the poor. The rich don't even have time for TV.

Planning is paramount to building success and becoming wealthy. It is the key that turns a dream to reality. It is a top secret of achievement the rich don't tell. Don't tell them I told you!

3) They make sure their income remains higher than their expenses.

This should make sense right? Of course it does. Anyone that spends more than he earns is not wise and will never become wealthy. Making sure your income remains higher than your expenses is the begging of wisdom. Well, credit card companies will not like me now but the truth is they make a lot of money on your ignorance, which is why they spend billions of dollars on marketing and ad campaigns to make you believe your life will be miserable without the stuffs you desire, even if you can't avoid them now. Just so you should take credit. It is so bad that most American households today have consumer debts and the banks are busy enriching their self's with those high interest rates. You should do your best to avoid debts and live within your means.

It isn't easy to live within your means especially when you have a low income, but you have to find a way around it. Look closely and fish out stuffs you don't need but you spend money on, and unnecessary expenses of eating out, travelling and entertainments. You won't die if these luxuries wait for the mean time. Begin to find pleasure in cooking, reading, using public transport and watching free channels. Ignore the

Joneses and stop trying to impress people. People don't really care what you do.

Making sure your income remain higher than your expenses is a simply calculation principle anyone with a basic education can practice without having a need to pay a professional for it. Expenses are moneys that goes out from you, be it in cash or dept it is gone and will never come back except in case of an investment, while income is the moneys that comes to you. Wealthy people when growing wealth had the sense to cut off unnecessary expense and make sure they made do of what they earn. Not just that, they also made sure to safe a percentage of every penny they earned and used it in the expansion of their businesses and investing in new ideas.

4) They are innovative.

It is said that ideas rule the world. The wealthy understands it and will go to the extent of paying people to think for them just to be at the cutting edge and to be 21th centaury complaint. They understand that times change and seasons come and go. So they move with time and change in season. You can never keep such a fellow on the spot.

Innovation is easily confused with invention and I will love you get the difference. Innovation isn't strictly creating something new; it is the ability to come up with a better idea or method in what you do and this can be applied in various perspectives even to simple things like how you fold your cloths. From a business perspective, you should be able to come up with better ways to improve customer satisfaction, reduce costs and increase productivity. Surround yourself with innovative people, people that can come up with better ideas to help you stand-out in your career or business.

Ideas rule the world and if you don't work in it forget success. Everything you see, use and enjoy today was as a result of someone's idea. The cars we drive, the phones we use, the cloths we ware, our coffee cups are all as a result of someone's idea. A lot of these stuffs have made life easier and is making the world a better place. People are solving the numerous problems of mankind and getting paid handsomely for it. The more problem you solve the more money you make. You do not have to be Bill Gates or Steve Jobs. You do not even have to change the world. All you have to do is constantly find ways to change your own small world by making your carrier or business better than the usual.

Henry Ford of the Ford Motor Company did not invent the automobile neither did he invent the assembly line but he is responsible for transforming the automobile industry with his innovation to make production faster and easier. And in 1913 he developed a moving assembly line for automobiles, revolutionizing the assembly line usual way of production.

5) They are self-confident.

I leant the story of a man who got a job not too far from the street where he lived if he uses the short cut (foot paths in between houses). It was dream come true, he was excited because he didn't have to spend on transport. First day to work, he got up early had his breakfast, got set and headed for the short cut. To his greatest amazement was a 3ft tall brown big old bull dog lying on the path, "damn" he exclaimed. The bull dog lifted up its big old red eyes and when they made eyes contact the man turned 180 degrees and got out of the place in the speed of light. "Shit... shit... he said panting, I'm never going to go back their again! He took a taxi that day and continued to take taxi to work for about 3 months until one day. It was a special day; it was a day that was going set off the beginning of better days in his career. He was to make a presentation to the board of directors of this mega organization he was working for. Here he was standing in front of his apartment with a brief case and an A3 file containing five sheets of his graphical presentation drawings, and for some reason no taxi on sight. He was already running late and it dawned on him that foot path he visited three months ago is his only option to make it to the office in good time. Recalling his experience with the big old red eyes bull dog his heart began to race but he had no option as the dog was the only thing standing in between him and greatness so he decided to summon courage and face his fair. Taking that bend once again was the 3ft tall brown big old bull dog lying on the path; "damn" he exclaimed as usual, the bull dog lifted up its big old red eyes, he stood there still he could hardly hear his self breath with ghost pimples all over his body, the bull dog started growling as its eyes bulged out and it began to bark, to his greatest shock this scary big old bull dog have no teeth's. His worse night mare was only a toothless bull dog. And from that day on he made use of the foot path and learned to be confident to face his fairs.

I dare to say, you need a little bit of stubbornness to attain a satin level of success. Courage, self believe and confidence. You've got to go against all odds, to accomplish new goals. Not minding what people are saying, and sometimes ignoring so called facts because your instinct says yes!

Successful people believe in their self's like a little boy believes in his daddy. They never say I cannot do it, they say I can do it! They never say it is not possible, they say how can I make it possible? You must have to programme your mind to operate in the positive and do away with people that constantly bring a negative energy around you, and surround yourself with people that lift your spirit.

Self confidence is a vital quality to a successful career. It's one of the core foundations you must develop to attain success and build wealth.

You must believe in yourself for people to believe in you.

6) They source information from those who do it well and use the system that works best.

Smart people learn from their mistakes, smarter people learn from other peoples mistakes. If the earth is 4.543 billion years old today according to scientists and a population of 7.125 billion humans lives on it. There is nothing you are trying to do that has not in an exact or a different form been done by someone already, as most things in life are products of recreation.

The fastest and easiest way of getting to a destination is to simply follow the steps of those who have made it successfully to that destination. That way, you will be able to learn from their costly mistakes and experiences, and will enjoy the advantage to save time and money. Device means to hook up with people that have gone where you are trying to go so you may ask questions, listen and pick their brains. Take advantage of every lunch and coffee break, send them little gifts, always complement them and write them a thank you note every time they give you audience. It is paramount that you build authentic and genuine relationship them. This kind of people are called mentors, and there is such a thing as distance mentors if you are not privileged to dine with them, you can study them, know how they operate, how they run they business, how they manage people, how they handle challenges and how they take decisions. Read every book they write, follow them on social media and constantly look them up on their websites, you will understand their system.

Successful people just find the best people in their line of business copy the system and customise it. By doing so they by-pass all try and error stages, failure stages and loss processes. It is a very smart principle successful people use for lots of their achievements. They source information from those who do it well and use the system that works best.

7) They are not limited by what they know, they focus on opportunities.

In other words they don't stick to one thing or just one source of income only. They hunt for fresh opportunities and invest in them beside what they originally do. Wealth creators don't say I don't know Computers so I will stick to my Agriculture. If you behave like that, you will one day be described as that fellow who used to be a millionaire. Because time moves and seasons change so you might be holding on to a sinking ship. Few years ago the stock exchange was a boom but today social media is what is trending. The fact that iphone is trending today don't mean it is going to trend forever. Many other old mobile phone companies used to trend like that but like I said time moves and seasons change. You must enlarge your horizon and focus on new opportunities constantly.

It is not that the rich are Jacks of all trade, no; they just make sure they have multiple streams of income. They know how to source for information, hire expatriates and delegate duties. As it does not only upgrade their financial status for a better lifestyle but also to establish financial security. Having just one source of income is a risky way to live. Today there are high rates of unemployment and job losses everywhere around the world, so even if you feel you have a very good job you are still not safe, the fact is nobody relying on a job for their livelihood is safe. So, even if you won't do it for luxury you still have to do it for security.

Cornelius Vanderbilt who became one of the wealthiest Americans of the 19th century was a Shipping tycoon and in 1860 saw an opportunity in Railroad sold out majority of his shipping empire and shifted his focus to the railroad industry where he successfully built another empire. Always remember that wealthy people focus on opportunities and not just what they know.

8) They take calculated risk.

One of the richest men in the world today, Bill Gates an American born on October 28, 1955 took a huge risk while founding Microsoft. He had to drop out of college and also dropped every other thing he had going on to create Microsoft. He was prepared to face the unexpected and follow his vision no matter the consequences. Fortunately, Bill succeeded to archive his goal and have succeeded not to only change his life but changed the world.

Have you ever wondered if Bill would have chosen to play save. Go to school, get good grades and get a job like everyone else if he would have revolutionized the world with his awesome computer software technology? Of course not, he would have been some ordinary guy living in some city, struggling with finances.

Risk implies the chance that things might not work out the way you expect. But, Go for it and you might succeed, leave it and you have failed. The qualm is that fear is holding you back, and fear is a dream killer. Don't let your fear of failure stop you from reaching your full potential. Don't let it arrest your mind. It could play at the outside but never let it get to your inside. Interpret failure as a valuable learning experience, that way, you will deal with the temptation to play save.

Average people always want to play save. They ask questions like "What if it doesn't work out?" instead of questions like "How can it work out?" So they get griped with fair and you hear them say things like "My job isn't so bad!" and their whole creative ability gets weaken automatically.

Big risks comes with big results, don't hesitate to take that bold step if you've paid attention to the details of how things are going to work out. Refuse to be comfortable with mediocrity. Wealthy people don't do that. They always go for it once the vision is clear!

9) They are committed.

Life's most valuable stuffs are rare. They are always in scares quantities and not easy to find. So is commitment.

Put before me a committed person and a talented person and I will go for the committed person because a committed person will write that exams again, apply that job again and try that business again. Commitment can get you anything in life and help you keep it because you earned it. It can get you where you want to be, no deliberation. It always does the magic. Every rightfully committed person I know is successful but I have met gifted people that their life is still a mess. Successful people are very committed people. They never seize to show up; they are always with a steadfast fixity. They've got what I call the "stay on it ability".

A lot of people have been left behind in the pursuit of the good things of life due to the lack of commitment and some of them are extremely talented people but the lack of commitment is killing them. Talented, yes they are. Successful, no they are not. The lack of commitment is keeping them on the spot. And the worst thing that can happen to a fellow is to be at the spot while the world is moving. Take a look at a stagnant river, it stink's and grow all sorts of unpleasant bacteria but a flowing river is flourishing, fresh and delightful.

Commitment starts with clarity of vision then a push of one's self to the course of action with serious mindedness and earnestness until your goal is archived. Sacrificing your time, money and pleasure. And sometimes even relationships.

Most times commitments are products of hard times and challenges. So don't feel bad of your challenges or how bad someone is treating you, instead use it as a motivation. That's what successful people do; they turn stumbling stones into stepping stones.

10) They are organized.

Successful people are together, well structured and organized. They know what to do, when to do it and how to do it. If they where your friends you can't just walk up to them and request to hang–out like you do with ordinary friends. This guys have what we call schedules and this schedules could be occupied for the whole year. O yeah! That is why they are very productive because it helps them to be more focused on what they want to achieve and gives them the ability to manage their time more effectively.

You must understand that success is intentional; you must be deliberate about it. It isn't something you bump into on the streets of London or New York. Neither can you go to the store to price a 2017 model. You won't find it available for sale anywhere in the world. You have to work it to earn it. Put yourself together, prepare your moves, and organize yourself. Keep track of your papers and appointments; make space for your keys, wallet, charger cables and stuffs you make use of from time to time to reduce stress, safe time and increase efficiency. So when you need something you know exactly where to find it.

To some people organization is just part of their personality; others were influenced by their parents when they were younger, while others develop it in the course of their carrier. When they began to receive more than the number of calls they can handle, more orders to process, more clients to attained to, more cheques to balance, etc. Whichever the case getting organized is paramount. It is the key of operation to any establishment that has succeeded. Wealthy people take organization very seriously.

CHAPTER 2

10 MONEY IDEOLOGIES YOU MUST CHANGE

1) "I don't want much; I just want to be comfortable"

I understand that they are really nice flocks that don't want to look selfish. So they decide not to go for more in life because it seems to them like they want everything to them self alone. This people don't want to be greedy, they just want enough to be comfortable. In other words, they wish and plan to be average, thinking abundance is greed. Abundance isn't greed my friend, it is security. You must put to consideration the fact that economic climates do change and they could have contractions. What will you do when business go bad? Or when you lose your job?

Stop being comfortable living on pay-check to pay-check. Always have an allowance and go for more. Mediocrity sucks! It shuts down your mind to do better and leaves you vulnerable to little challenges.

Other people developed this wrong ideology from religious misconceptions, while others are just lazy. I don't know what your faith is, but I do know that God wants you in good health and prosperity. Lazy people will always find a way to justify their condition. They will always give reasons for failing and giving up. Why in the world will you choose to pass the baton of poverty your father passed to you to your children? And you will leave another generation in hardship. Some of us where not born with a silver spoon but we created one, and our children will be born with it.

If you love your phone fully charged, and your car on full gauge why not an extra income and bigger savings. Wanting more is not being selfish, on the contrary not wanting more is being selfish, because you can't help other people. How can you give when you just have enough for yourself? Think about how many lives' you can touch when you have a little bit just more then you need. They thousands of orphanage children you can supply food and medical health care. The poor people in Africa that still don't have access to clean drinking water and quality education. Think about it! Your extra income could save lives.

2) "I have got to make money to be rich"

Making money requires time and effort but gaining money necessary don't. The ideology of making money will limit you in wealth creation. You will be focused on what you can do, instead of what your money can do. For example, employees work for money. They make money only when they show up to exchange their time and effort for a check. Imagine how many times you will have to show up to become rich. This should give you a second thought if you think it is my your straight. You will just grow old and weary.

Business owners and investors don't have to make money; they pay people to make money for them. Every day you go to work you make money for your boss. If your boss decides not to go to the office he still makes money, when he is sleeping he still makes money, if he decides to go on a three months vacation to the Bahamas to bask his self on gorgeous powdery white beaches and swim in pristine turquoise waters he still makes money, and not just from you but from every other employee on his or her pay roll. Never forget this; you cannot enter into financial freedom working for someone including yourself. You can only come into riches having quite a hand full of people working for you and having your money working for you.

If you have to fill a water tank with a tea cup all alone, it will take you hundred's of days of exhaustion, that's if you don't get frustrated and give up, but when you've got about a hundred people with tea cups filling the tank. In no time you would have a full tank and an ample of time to enjoy your success. "The strength of many people is more than the strength of a strong man". No wonder even the Holy book says, one will chase a thousand and two can ten thousand.

3) "More money, more problems"

If this phrase is correct how come everyone still wants more money knowing that it will only amount to more problems? More money don't amount to more problems, more money amount to quality problems. Get the difference!

I always ask people, I say the month you make extra money do you have more problems that month? And the answer is always an emphatic no. I'm like how in the world then did you fall into these mental money trap that more money creates more problems! Then I discovered that people who say it are broke people, all the rich guys I know are willing to make more money and are planning to make sure that their children's children are born in wealth.

More money helps you solve your old embarrassing problems and create new kinds of problems. Problems rich people have, problems like where to Bank your billions, which country to go shopping, should I buy a Bugatti or Ferrari, where do I pack my private jet and of course, the problem of having to hire two pilots and a mechanic for the jet. These problems, I will gladly accept. They are quality problems everyone will love to have. The problems are lovely. Whereby the problem at hand is the problem of choice, which colour do I buy? Forget the price tags.

More money more problems is phase the masses use to justify being broke. Don't fall for it, don't say it. More money means quality problems not more problems.

4) "It takes money to make money"

Did you know that majority of the billionaires the world celebrate today are self-made? They were ordinary people and some of them came from poor backgrounds. Forbes said, almost 300, to be exact 273 that made its 400 Billionaires list are self-made, they scrapped their way into the list through their own efforts. Bill Gates, Warren Buffett, Amancio Ortega of Zara, Larry Ellison of Oracle, Jeff Bezos of Amazon, Ingvar Kamprad, Carlos Slim, Mark Zuckerberg to mention just a few, you think used money to make all those billions they have? No! They had an idea, made a plan, took on courage, moved in action and remained persistent. These were what they used to generate wealth and not money, besides they had no money. So, if it truly takes money to make money we won't be talking about them right now.

First, what you need is an Idea. The smarter your idea the bigger your chances, some ideas are worth a million dollars, some are ten thousand and another may worth billions. The question is what problem are you solving? People want to get rich but are unwilling to pay the price. No one will want to give you money; you've got to come up with smart legal means to force the money out of them. I remember one of the leading computer manufacturing companies who didn't like Bill Gates, they rejected Bill's proposal to install Microsoft on their computers, but Bill didn't fret, he went on to make Microsoft the best operating system at the time, and this computer manufacturing company didn't like Bill Gates but there had to call him back to purchase the Microsoft operating system for all their computers if they don't want to go out of business, because everyone wanted a computer with the Microsoft operating system.

When you make yourself relevant people may not like your face but babe you are indispensable, their will look for you to give you money. Just solve a problem. Secondly, you need a plan on how to execute your idea. Where to start from, people to meet and how you will operate. Finally, take action by following your plan like a jealous lover and begin to execute them step by step, one after another, bit by bit like you have programmed.

Persist, keep the pressure and always remember that "winners don't quit and quitters don't win".

5) "Money don't grow on trees"

Is this phrase literally true? Yes it is true that money don't literally grow on trees, leaves do. But is the morale behind the phrase true? No, it's not. The phrase money don't grow on trees is suggesting that money is almost impossible and very difficult to find, meaning it is limited and scare. Believe this phrase and you will toil for the rest of your life.

This is a terrible ideology for people trying to create wealth and gain financial freedom. It will be the beginning of their failure. You must realise that your mind is your most powerful weapon. It is the primary battle ground to creating success and growing wealth, that's where it all starts and end. Believe that you won't make it, guess what? You won't. Believe that you can, and you will. The mind is powerful, that is why you must sanitize what you hear, and the people you listen to. People you keep around you and people you hang-out with. Your mind must be kept positive at all cost.

Money is everywhere. It is in every city, forest and sea. That's how you should see it. Your perspective must be right and your believe should be positive, because whatever you believe you will attract. Believe that money is difficult to find, it sure would be difficult for you. Believe that money is easy to find and your eyes will light up to see opportunities.

Money, the most common medium of exchange is only a finished product of Ideas, services rendered or materials sold. It is important that you begin to see these things as moneys waiting to be transformed into the official currency issued by the government or banks. This means that money is all over, in the ground, on the ground, in the sea and even in the air.

6) "Another day, another dollar"

The average person believes that the only way to make money is to work more. He believes that you should take a second job, work more hours and more days if you need more money. His method is to exchange his time for money not realising that you can only have so much of it. 365 days is all you've got in a year and the average life expectancy is around 45 to 85 depending on your country.

Never count in days in your mission of wealth creation. Let every second count even when you are at sleep, and let the next day be better than the previous day. You should have a mindset of increase; make sure you keep getting better day by day, and let your finances grow. If you work in a place with a very slow pace of promotion quit the job, it is not a good place to build a career.

The rich exchange dollars for your time when they employ you, because they value time more than money. They know how precious time is. So, they hire people for their time and pay them just enough to come back the next day.

The Acts of Wealth Creation

Refuse to be limited by days, months or years in creating wealth. Value every second of your life, make good use of it and sell it not.

7) "Money is the root of all evil"

Money cannot be the root of all evil. The actual saying is "the love of money is the root of all evil".

It befouls me how people have allowed money to blend fold them with its power. They fail to realise that money is just a medium of exchange that should be used by men and not the other way round. The heart of men is what is evil, money is just a currency. It has no emotion, it has no feelings, it plans neither evil nor good. It is what its master wants it to be. Put money in the hands of a good man and you will see good deeds in full measure, and put money in the hands of an evil man and you will see evil deeds in full measure. I have told people times without number that money don't change people, money only brings out the true character in people. You know human beings can pretend.

Those who worship money will do evil for it, but those who have learnt to put money in its place don't have a fertile land of heart where evil seeds can grow.

When a fellow is desperate and begins to do anything for money is when evil crawls in and money is being abused. Abuse is an act of misusing something or somebody. That means changing the inherent purpose of something. Money is a good thing and has the capability to perform a lot of things. Find it, make it, and use it, but never fall in love it.

Moneys are indispensable commodities in human lives and should not be underrated or misunderstood. It is important that you have financial education and you teach your kids how it works, because it is life. From food to shelter, health to clothing, education to entertainment money does it all. It sets the standard of a lifestyle. If you will have to eat only what you can afford or what you want to eat. If you will have to live with a roommate, in a flat, or own your own mansion with a pool, a Jacuzzi, and a private bowling court. If your kids will attained the best of schools and have a great start for a bright future or attained public schools. It will enable you support people, help your community, make donations and give to charity. Money will determine the kind of life you will live. Be the good hands it comes to.

Money is good and very important. It is not the root of all evil; the love of money is the root of all evil.

8) "A penny saved is a penny earned"

Have this mind set and you will never become rich. A cousin of mine said this to me one day, I stared at him for a moment shook my head left and right and I said "no wonder you are still broke."

Saving pennies will never get you rich but old. Yeah, I said it. If you like live a hundred and twenty you will never attain financial freedom. No one ever got rich saving money, they just got old trying. Savings is good but don't focus on it, focus on creating wealth. Tell me one rich person you know who got rich saving money? Not one, because they all got rich making money and having people and their money make money for them.

The phrase "a penny saved is a penny earned" is an ideology of the masses. Scared of losing their hard earned money they go to the bank to keep money in fix deposits and savings accounts, and the banks use their money to do business for gain and also loan it to rich people for interest to expand their businesses. So, technically the moneys masses save are the moneys rich people borrow to expand their businesses and employ more masses.

You have to change your way of thinking if you really want to become wealthy. Quit thinking about saving pennies and start thinking about making millions.

9) "Money can't buy happiness"

Happiness is a journey of moments, and not a destination. It is not a commodity you can find on the shelf of a super market or a mega shopping mall. It is a feeling that can be created with or without money. When you are blessed with a child, money did not buy you the child, but when you are blessed with a car, money bought you the car. Money can create lots of happy moments and so does God's natural gifts, a forgiving heart and a positive attitude. I recommend you enjoy happiness on all sides.

God's gift's is one source of happiness. The air we breathe, the beautiful sky, the birds of the air, the huge mountains, the oceans, the lovely trees and flowers, the animals, the rain and snow can all be a source of happiness for mankind if a man opens his eyes to see the beauty of creation. You must also have a forgiving heart no matter what someone must have done to you, because forgiveness is not really for the person that has offended you but it is for you. It is for your peace of mind, dropping all that heaviness, pain and bitterness will make you smile again, love again and live again.

I don't know about you, but as for me I am happier when I have money in pocket and bank accounts.

The Acts of Wealth Creation

When I don't have to worry on how I'm going to pay the mortgage, school fees and medical health care. When my heart don't race and begin to do somehow. I am happier when I can pay my bills, help the people I love, shop without limit, and afford the things I need. Money is the commodity that can make this things happen. So, to some extent money can make you happy. But never forget that money can't do everything for you, no matter how much you have and in what so ever currency you have them money cannot buy life, money cannot give you salvation.

10) "Rich people are stingy"

I'm sick and tired of hearing people say, "if I had his money I would help so many people", and I'm like, "what the hack are you waiting for?" Most of them are dead broke and don't even have a plan to get their own self out of poverty. They live life thinking about what they will do, and not what they can do. Do you think that rich people don't like praises and accolades? Of course they do. It is just that riches come with a price. They had to instinct discipline to their life's by controlling unnecessary spending, cutting down living expenses and depriving their self's and the people around them the little pleasures of life everybody is enjoying because they understand the principle of saving to invest. They had to discipline their self's with reckless spending to be able to invest, expand and grow their business. That was how they go rich.

So, it isn't that rich people are stingy; they are just disciplined with money. An overweight airplane can't fly and so an overweight person. Not necessarily in physical but in carrying responsibilities. For example, taking a wife and having kids when you hardly fend for your self is signing a life contract with Dr. Lack and Mr. Poverty, because you will hardly have extra income to save, invest and grow your business. It will always be from one financial need to another, debts will begin to pile up and you will be hooked forever. I like to use the analogy of mountain climbers for men of vision. The mountain is your vision, how and when you will get to the peak all depends on you. Mountain climbers don't climb the mountain with heavy loads; they travel with only what they will need. A backpack, helmet, boots, crampons and some few more stuffs. They don't take everything and everybody along. What or who have you been trying to carry to the top that is slowing your pace?

It is easier to pull people to the top when you are at the top, than to carrying them up from the ground. Believe me, the higher your mountain (vision) the lighter you will want to make your load.

CHAPTER 3

10 HABITS YOU MUST CULTIVATE

1) Read relentlessly

The world is moving so fast that you have to be on your "A-game" to keep up. New technologies are evolving and things are changing on a daily basis. How businesses are being run, operations, logistics, governance and so on.

You must set yourself on auto update, improve daily and be 21st centaury compliant to be relevant. It doesn't matter your career, whether it is Entertainment, Politics, Business, Sports or Education, you have to be at the cutting edge to triumph. And this can only be achieved by studying. Read relentlessly gives your brain a special kind of workout, it develops your brain, boosts your vocabulary, reduces stress, and improves your memory, empathy, focus and concentration. The more you read, the more knowledge you will have and the better equipped you will be. In fact, reading keeps your brain young according to Rush University Medical Centre study report. Adults who spent their downtime doing creative or intellectual activities like reading had a 32% slower rate of cognitive decline later in life than those who did not.

Dedicate time to reading blogs, news papers, magazines and books. Read every good material you find, it will help you stimulate your thought processes, increase your intelligence and expand your horizon. But most of all read for self-improvement, study materials that will help you fan your skills to flame.

Never let a day go by without improving yourself in your line of work. This doesn't necessarily means reading for hours or crushing an entire book in one day, but putting aside a little time to read every day. You can start by skimming through materials for about 20 to 30 minutes every day and thank goodness for audio books nowadays, listen to them in traffic and during the commute to work.

2) Exercise

Your health is your most valuable asset. Be the most successful person in the world, it won't matter if you don't have good health.

Exercising is a habit you will want to develop if you want to work productivity and live to enjoy what you have laboured for. It is a miracle dose you must learn to take on daily bases. Regardless of age, exercising boost your brain function, self-esteem, energy, sleep quality and mood, as well as reduce stress and the risk of illnesses such as stroke, heart disease, diabetes and even cancer.

Exercising doesn't have to be working out for hours. It just requires physical activities from you on daily basis. Nowadays people are less active. We drive air conditioned cars and no more walk. We use the elevators, shop online and have the machines wash our clothes. We avoid all the manual work and house chores. This causes us to move around less and burn off fewer calories than required. A body that consumes 2500 calories a day but burns only 2000 calories daily will definitely gain weight. Increased physical activity will help you manage weight and enjoy the numerous health benefits, like building a stronger heart and lungs to improve blood flow and deliver more oxygen and nutrients throughout the body. It also results to increased stamina, stronger bones and built muscle tissues.

Make it a habit to be physically active. If you can't hit the gym every day, walk short distance instead of using the car and take the stairs instead of the elevator. What is required is that you move quickly enough to raise your heart rate, breathe faster and feel warmer.

3) Eat healthy

Like a car needs a quality fuel and regular good engine oil change and maintenance to function effectively and last long, so does our bodies need a healthy diet to get the right balance of vitamins, minerals and other nutrients to support optimal health. A good diet is the fuel our body consume for good health and energy. Just like the car, if you don't use quality fuel for it and change to a good engine oil time to time it will definitely begin to have problems and soon go off road.

Healthy eating will prevent and control many health problems such as, Heart disease, type (2) diabetes, high blood pressure and many more health issues. It will help you maintain a healthy weight, look good and feel better. It improves your overall well being benefiting your physical, mental and emotional health.

As a potential multimillionaire trust me you don't have time to be sick or money to throw around on health issues you could have avoided. Eating healthy isn't always easy, but you've got to make it a habit if you really want to have the right energy you need to create wealth and a long life to enjoy it. Aim to consume a diet rich in fruits, vegetables, unsaturated fats and whole grains. Rarely consume foods that are high in sodium, saturated fat and added sugar. Stay hydrated and don't skip meals. It is no new news that busy people work through lunch and sometimes sleep through breakfast. I still fight that challenge as it could not only cause an energy drain but also lowered nutrition and risk for some diseases. Our body needs a steady supply of nutrients to maintain functionality and intellectuality.

4) Sleep moderately

Sleep plays a very vital role in our general well being. Our bodies are like machines; they work very hard and needs to be given some time to rest. While asleep your brain and body is fixing itself from the rigours of day to day life. It benefits your body and your mind.

Do you know that a good night rest can even determine if you will have a good or bad day? I discovered that any day I have adequate sleep my day was more productive. I will be fresh, happier and active. It enables me to relate with my clients more friendly. It just makes me feel better, so I work better.

People who lack enough sleep won't just risk developing chronic health problems, but have high tendency to get frustrated on little tasks at work and get mad on the slightest issues. Sleep affects how you think, react, work and learn.

But in as much as sleeping is very important to your physical health and state of mind, it shouldn't be overdone, it should be done moderately, wisely and timely. People who sleep for 8 hours a day sleep a total of 122 days a year. So by the time you are 60 years old you have spent 20 years of your life sleeping.

You must budget how long you sleep and when you sleep. Time is a respecter of no one and will not wait a second for you to have a break. So, you must learn to spend it wisely and make the best use of it. Your action between sunrise and sunset today and always shapes your bank account. Trust me don't want to spend majority of your time in bed.

5) Schedule your day

Never start a day without a schedule; it is your key to productivity and time management. A lot of things could get you distracted and some other things you might give too much time to than necessary. Schedule puts you on the watch. You will be able to allocate time judiciously even at this era of social media and lots of unproductive activities. Have you ever thought of making a call only to realise that the day was gone and you haven't put the call through? Because you got busy engaged in other things and probably forgot or just kept on postponing. Some people have taken weeks to get few hours task done that way, wasting precious time.

The world today is said to be in *the **Age of Information*** but permit me to add ***and of distraction***. Except you are wise you will be easily distracted from what you need to focus on. The Internet, Games, Television, Endless Party, Alcohol and even drug abuse are obvious distractions from what we need to focus on to better our lives and benefit the society.

Having a set schedule is a powerful tool to avoiding distractions and making the most of your day. Successful people are sticklers for schedule. They go to sleep at about the same time every night and wake up at about the same time every morning. They allot time to tasks and make sure they get it done, that's why they are successful.

Keeping a schedule is the best way to extinguish and annihilate the temptation of procrastination which is one of the major deterrents to productivity. Make your schedule the day before, this way the moment you wake up at morning you will know just what to do and when to do it.

You must also come to the cognisance that activity is not productivity. So, every activity without productivity is nonsense.

6) Always be on time

Whatever your appointment or engagement, punctuality demonstrates that you are diligent, committed and dependable. It shows you can be trusted. Believe me you will need your clients to have that impression about you.

Nowadays most people are habitually late for everything. For work, religious meeting, social gathering and even for their child's school events. In Africa it has even been given a name "African time", people will deliberately stay at home until it is pass the appointment, event or meeting time before they begin their journey to the venue. It is so annoying and I laugh at those people when I hear them say they want to succeed, go places and become relevant. I will be like, seriously! "You can never make it with this attitude". Because I know that one of the attributes of successful people is that they value and respect time. Personally, one thing I never play with is my reputation. I always try to maintain an excellent reputation, lead by example and create a great image everywhere I go.

It is so important to be on time for your appointments, as it will also give you few minutes to relax, put yourself together and think about your agenda. Plan to always show up on time, include your transit time and possible traffic delays. At least arrive 5 to 10 minutes earlier.

7) Always Go the Extra Mile

It doesn't matter if you are a business owner or an employee. Going the extra mile will always pull the attention of your clients or superiors. If you should drop your car at a service shop for wheel balancing and aliments, and you were asked to come back in an hour. Only to be back and see that the wheel balancing is done, aliments are perfectly set and the car is also been washed and you could smell a sweet flavour deodorant, all in 45 minutes. "Wow" I'm pretty sure you must be tempted to ask me where to find this service workshop. Not only will you go back again and again, but you will tell all your friends of this amazing car service shop you have found. How the guys did your wheel balancing and aliments so well and how an extra treat was added, the washing, good smell and all of that.

This is one phenomenal thing going the extra mile can do for you, "free advertisement". People will not only advertise you but also will recommend you to other people. The will have confidence in what you do. Everyone wants great products and services.

Whatever you do, don't stop at what is required of you. People don't appreciate what is expected especially when they pay for it. Do a few more extra tasks, work an hour extra, be your boss number one problem solver, and even if you have to present a problem present it with a solution. If you are an employee work an extra hour, if you are a service provider give a free special offer, if you are an event planner, add an extra table, an extra flower, an extra decoration and so on.

Whatever you do, just make sure to always go extra mile, do more than your job or contracts requires of you.

8) Save (to invest)

I will always say it, that savings don't get people rich, creating wealth do. The only reason you should save is to invest. Never use your savings to buy a TV, a phone, a Car or even pay bills. That's a whole lot of money that can go into work for you. Remember that you can never be rich working for someone including yourself, you must be able to put your money and other people to work for you so when you are not their you still make money. Buy Treasury Bills and enjoy its generous return, buy a cute home and put it out for rent, buy Bonds. Invest in smart people's business ideas. I know of people who made millions of dollars investing in people's businesses. Ben Horowitz made over $78 million in 2012 investing only $250,000 in Instagram and also counts Twitter and Skype among his success stories. David Choe made over $200 million investing just $60,000 in Facebook. Imagine you invested just $10,000 in Amazon, Dell, Apple, or Microsoft when they went IPO, you would be in millions right now, without having to be the founder or do all the work. Whether you are investing a lump sum of money from your built up savings or investing a smaller amount in a monthly savings plan. Investment will always change your financial circumstance over time.

Your money can always go to work while you relax or do other things. And the best way you can invest is to save. Money will never jump on your laps and say "here am I invest me!" You will have to take a deliberate action to always save a little from little. Open a sacred account and keep depositing part of your every income. Personally I (Save 30%, pay a Tithe of 10% and Spend 60%) of my every income. You can make an adjustment to what plan fit's you best and be committed to your financial plan no matter what it takes. Commit to growing your savings, investment opportunities will always come around.

9) Be a friendly person

Whatever you do, if you like jump up and come down the moneys you make come from people. There is nothing as "new money", every money is belonging to an individual, an organisation or the government. The only place money is fund is with people. Even if you mine diamonds you need someone to buy them.

A good relationship for successful people cannot be over emphasized. Relationship with your clients, staffs, friends and family, all drives your success. They are the people that will support you, pray for you, encourage you, patronize you, market you and bail you out in times of trouble. Being friendly builds relationships. People want to feel appreciated and respected. It has a way of brings out the best in them.

You've got to be amiable. Know how to meet people, make new friends and show love. Ask questions, get to know how the people around you are faring, and support them how you can. Learn nice jokes and share it time to time, don't be too zealous all the time, as this will mend your relationship with your staffs, clients or customers. Be affable when you go to places, and always leave them with the impression that, "that fellow is a really nice person", and when next you go back you will be amazed of the warmth welcome you will receive and how quickly things will be done for you.

I know you can't please everyone, that's just how life is. But always make efforts. Being nice is for you, and so is forgiveness.

10) Always aim high

People who get into the habit of dreaming big accomplish most of their goals because they have the right mindset. Having the right mindset is the coolest thing that can happen to you on your journey to creating wealth. It is your most powerful weapon to success. Guide it with all your heart. People will try to discourage you from setting big-goal, they will make statements like, "Be realistic", the next time those words are thrown at you, take a look at your goals again, and if what you are aiming for can be done by a human being or a group of people, then your goal is possible, and if it is possible it is realistic. Ignore the fellow and never tell him or her about your dreams again. Success starts with your ability to believe in yourself and in your vision. Never let anyone talk you out of it.

Aiming high will raise your performance to a level you wouldn't ordinarily attain. For example, if a student aims to make an "A" in his exams and face a little challenge it will not drop him too far, probably a "B", but if he aims for a "C" and unfortunately encounters a challenge he is going to be in real trouble.   High aims will cause a practical impact on your drive. It will make you push yourself and force you to do more. You will become extensively creative because your body system will respond to the task at hand and begin to work at its highest level of creativity. Even those who work with you will be motivated. Daniel Burnham said, *"Make no small plans; they have no magic to stir men's souls."*

Set goals that scare you and do whatever it takes to hit your target and even if you fall you won't fall too low.

www.ingramcontent.com/pod-product-compliance
Lightning Source LLC
Chambersburg PA
CBHW021441170526
45164CB00001B/341